A FURTHER RANGE

BOOK SIX

A
FURTHER
RANGE

BY

ROBERT

FROST

HENRY HOLT AND COMPANY

NEW YORK

Copyright, 1936, by Robert Frost

Printed in the United States of America

To E. F.

for what it may mean to her that beyond the White
Mountains were the Green; beyond both were the
Rockies, the Sierras, and, in thought, the Andes and
the Himalayas — range beyond range even into the
realm of government and religion

Many of these poems have had the advantage of previous publication in The Saturday Review of Literature, The Yale Review, Poetry, Scribner's Magazine, The Virginia Quarterly Review, The Atlantic Monthly, The American Mercury, Books, Direction and The New Frontier. The author wishes to make grateful acknowledgment.

A Preface of Contents

TAKEN DOUBLY

TAKEN SINGLY

BUILD SOIL

AFTERTHOUGHT

TAKEN DOUBLY

A LONE STRIKER

The swinging mill bell changed its rate
To tolling like the count of fate,
And though at that the tardy ran,
One failed to make the closing gate.
There was a law of God or man
That on the one who came too late
The gate for half an hour be locked,
His time be lost, his pittance docked.
He stood rebuked and unemployed.
The straining mill began to shake.
The mill, though many, many eyed,
Had eyes inscrutably opaque;
So that he couldn't look inside
To see if some forlorn machine
Was standing idle for his sake.
(He couldn't hope its heart would break.)

And yet he thought he saw the scene:
The air was full of dust of wool.
A thousand yarns were under pull,
But pull so slow, with such a twist,
All day from spool to lesser spool,
It seldom overtaxed their strength;
They safely grew in slender length.
And if one broke by any chance,
The spinner saw it at a glance.
The spinner still was there to spin.

That's where the human still came in.
Her deft hand showed with finger rings
Among the harp-like spread of strings.
She caught the pieces end to end
And, with a touch that never missed,
Not so much tied as made them blend.
Man's ingenuity was good.
He saw it plainly where he stood,
Yet found it easy to resist.

He knew another place, a wood,
And in it, tall as trees, were cliffs;
And if he stood on one of these,
'Twould be among the tops of trees,
Their upper branches round him wreathing,
Their breathing mingled with his breathing.
If – if he stood! Enough of ifs!
He knew a path that wanted walking;
He knew a spring that wanted drinking;
A thought that wanted further thinking;
A love that wanted re-renewing.
Nor was this just a way of talking
To save him the expense of doing.
With him it boded action, deed.

The factory was very fine;
He wished it all the modern speed.
Yet, after all, 'twas not divine,
That is to say, 'twas not a church.

He never would assume that he'd
Be any institution's need.
But he said then and still would say
If there should ever come a day
When industry seemed like to die
Because he left it in the lurch,
Or even merely seemed to pine
For want of his approval, why
Come get him—they knew where to search.

TWO TRAMPS IN MUD TIME

Out of the mud two strangers came
And caught me splitting wood in the yard.
And one of them put me off my aim
By hailing cheerily "Hit them hard!"
I knew pretty well why he dropped behind
And let the other go on a way.
I knew pretty well what he had in mind:
He wanted to take my job for pay.

Good blocks of beech it was I split,
As large around as the chopping block;
And every piece I squarely hit
Fell splinterless as a cloven rock.
The blows that a life of self-control
Spares to strike for the common good
That day, giving a loose to my soul,
I spent on the unimportant wood.

The sun was warm but the wind was chill.
You know how it is with an April day
When the sun is out and the wind is still,
You're one month on in the middle of May.
But if you so much as dare to speak,
A cloud comes over the sunlit arch,
A wind comes off a frozen peak,
And you're two months back in the middle
    of March.

A bluebird comes tenderly up to alight
And fronts the wind to unruffle a plume,
His song so pitched as not to excite
A single flower as yet to bloom.
It is snowing a flake: and he half knew
Winter was only playing possum.
Except in color he isn't blue,
But he wouldn't advise a thing to blossom.

The water for which we may have to look
In summertime with a witching-wand,
In every wheelrut's now a brook,
In every print of a hoof a pond.
Be glad of water, but don't forget
The lurking frost in the earth beneath
That will steal forth after the sun is set
And show on the water its crystal teeth.

The time when most I loved my task
These two must make me love it more
By coming with what they came to ask.
You'd think I never had felt before
The weight of an ax-head poised aloft,
The grip on earth of outspread feet,
The life of muscles rocking soft
And smooth and moist in vernal heat.

Out of the woods two hulking tramps
(From sleeping God knows where last night,

But not long since in the lumber camps).
They thought all chopping was theirs of right.
Men of the woods and lumberjacks,
They judged me by their appropriate tool.
Except as a fellow handled an ax,
They had no way of knowing a fool.

Nothing on either side was said.
They knew they had but to stay their stay
And all their logic would fill my head:
As that I had no right to play
With what was another man's work for gain.
My right might be love but theirs was need.
And where the two exist in twain
Theirs was the better right–agreed.

But yield who will to their separation,
My object in living is to unite
My avocation and my vocation
As my two eyes make one in sight.
Only where love and need are one,
And the work is play for mortal stakes,
Is the deed ever really done
For Heaven and the future's sakes.

THE WHITE-TAILED HORNET

The white-tailed hornet lives in a balloon
That floats against the ceiling of the woodshed.
The exit he comes out at like a bullet
Is like the pupil of a pointed gun.
And having power to change his aim in flight,
He comes out more unerring than a bullet.
Verse could be written on the certainty
With which he penetrates my best defense
Of whirling hands and arms about the head
To stab me in the sneeze-nerve of a nostril.
Such is the instinct of it I allow.
Yet how about the insect certainty
That in the neighborhood of home and children
Is such an execrable judge of motives
As not to recognize in me the exception
I like to think I am in everything—
One who would never hang above a bookcase
His Japanese crepe-paper globe for trophy?
He stung me first and stung me afterward.
He rolled me off the field head over heels,
And would not listen to my explanations.

That's when I went as visitor to his house.
As visitor at my house he is better.
Hawking for flies about the kitchen door,
In at one door perhaps and out another,
Trust him then not to put you in the wrong.

He won't misunderstand your freest movements.
Let him light on your skin unless you mind
So many prickly grappling feet at once.
He's after the domesticated fly
To feed his thumping grubs as big as he is.
Here he is at his best, but even here –
I watched him where he swooped, he pounced, he
    struck;
But what he found he had was just a nailhead.
He struck a second time. Another nailhead.
"Those are just nailheads. Those are fastened down."
Then disconcerted and not unannoyed,
He stooped and struck a little huckleberry
The way a player curls around a football.
"Wrong shape, wrong color, and wrong scent,"
    I said.
The huckleberry rolled him on his head.
At last it was a fly. He shot and missed;
And the fly circled round him in derision.
But for the fly he might have made me think
He had been at his poetry, comparing
Nailhead with fly and fly with huckleberry:
How like a fly, how very like a fly.
But the real fly he missed would never do;
The missed fly made me dangerously skeptic.

Won't this whole instinct matter bear revision?
Won't almost any theory bear revision?
To err is human, not to, animal.

Or so we pay the compliment to instinct,
Only too liberal of our compliment
That really takes away instead of gives.
Our worship, humor, conscientiousness
Went long since to the dogs under the table.
And served us right for having instituted
Downward comparisons. As long on earth
As our comparisons were stoutly upward
With gods and angels, we were men at least,
But little lower than the gods and angels.
But once comparisons were yielded downward,
Once we began to see our images
Reflected in the mud and even dust,
'Twas disillusion upon disillusion.
We were lost piecemeal to the animals,
Like people thrown out to delay the wolves.
Nothing but fallibility was left us,
And this day's work made even that seem doubtful.

A BLUE RIBBON AT AMESBURY

Such a fine pullet ought to go
All coiffured to a winter show,
And be exhibited, and win.
The answer is this one has been—

And come with all her honors home.
Her golden leg, her coral comb,
Her fluff of plumage, white as chalk,
Her style, were all the fancy's talk.

It seems as if you must have heard.
She scored an almost perfect bird.
In her we make ourselves acquainted
With one a Sewell might have painted.

Here common with the flock again,
At home in her abiding pen,
She lingers feeding at the trough,
The last to let night drive her off.

The one who gave her ankle-band,
Her keeper, empty pail in hand,
He lingers too, averse to slight
His chores for all the wintry night.

He leans against the dusty wall,
Immured almost beyond recall,

A depth past many swinging doors
And many litter-muffled floors.

He meditates the breeder's art.
He has a half a mind to start,
With her for Mother Eve, a race
That shall all living things displace.

'Tis ritual with her to lay
The full six days, then rest a day;
At which rate barring broodiness
She well may score an egg-success.

The gatherer can always tell
Her well-turned egg's brown sturdy shell,
As safe a vehicle of seed
As is vouchsafed to feathered breed.

No human spectre at the feast
Can scant or hurry her the least.
She takes her time to take her fill.
She whets a sleepy sated bill.

She gropes across the pen alone
To peck herself a precious stone.
She waters at the patent fount.
And so to roost, the last to mount.

The roost is her extent of flight.
Yet once she rises to the height,

She shoulders with a wing so strong
She makes the whole flock move along.

The night is setting in to blow.
It scours the windowpane with snow,
But barely gets from them or her
For comment a complacent chirr.

The lowly pen is yet a hold
Against the dark and wind and cold
To give a prospect to a plan
And warrant prudence in a man.

A DRUMLIN WOODCHUCK

One thing has a shelving bank,
Another a rotting plank,
To give it cozier skies
And make up for its lack of size.

My own strategic retreat
Is where two rocks almost meet,
And still more secure and snug,
A two-door burrow I dug.

With those in mind at my back
I can sit forth exposed to attack
As one who shrewdly pretends
That he and the world are friends.

All we who prefer to live
Have a little whistle we give,
And flash, at the least alarm
We dive down under the farm.

We allow some time for guile
And don't come out for a while
Either to eat or drink.
We take occasion to think.

And if after the hunt goes past
And the double-barrelled blast

(Like war and pestilence
And the loss of common sense),

If I can with confidence say
That still for another day,
Or even another year,
I will be there for you, my dear,

It will be because, though small
As measured against the All,
I have been so instinctively thorough
About my crevice and burrow.

THE GOLD HESPERIDEE

Square Matthew Hale's young grafted appletree
Began to blossom at the age of five;
And after having entertained the bee,
And cast its flowers and all the stems but three,
It set itself to keep those three alive;
And downy wax the three began to thrive.

They had just given themselves a little twist
And turned from looking up and being kissed
To looking down and yet not being sad,
When came Square Hale with Let's see what we
   had;
And two was all he counted (one he missed);
But two for a beginning wasn't bad.

His little Matthew, also five years old,
Was led into the presence of the tree
And raised among the leaves and duly told,
We mustn't touch them yet, but see and see!
And what was green would by and by be gold.
Their name was called the Gold Hesperidee.

As regularly as he went to feed the pig
Or milk the cow, he visited the fruit,
The dew of night and morning on his boot.
Dearer to him than any barnyard brute,
Each swung in danger on its slender twig,
A bubble on a pipe-stem growing big.

Long since they swung as three instead of two—
One more, he thought, to take him safely through.
Three made it certain nothing Fate could do
With codlin moth or rusty parasite
Would keep him now from proving with a bite
That the name Gold Hesperidee was right.

And so he brought them to the verge of frost.
But one day when the foliage all went swish
With autumn and the fruit was rudely tossed,
He thought no special goodness could be lost
If he fulfilled at last his summer wish,
And saw them picked unbruised and in a dish,

Where they could ripen safely to the eating.
But when he came to look, no apples there
Under, or on the tree, or anywhere,
And the light-natured tree seemed not to care!
'Twas Sunday and Square Hale was dressed for
    meeting.
The final summons into church was beating.

Just as he was without an uttered sound
At those who'd done him such a wrong as that,
Square Matthew Hale took off his Sunday hat
And ceremoniously laid it on the ground,
And leaping on it with a solemn bound,
Danced slowly on it till he trod it flat.

Then suddenly he saw the thing he did,

And looked around to see if he was seen.
This was the sin that Ahaz was forbid
(The meaning of the passage had been hid):
To look upon the tree when it was green
And worship apples. What else could it mean?

God saw him dancing in the orchard path,
But mercifully kept the passing crowd
From witnessing the fault of one so proud.
And so the story wasn't told in Gath;
In gratitude for which Square Matthew vowed
To walk a graver man restrained in wrath.

IN TIME OF CLOUDBURST

Let the downpour roil and toil!
The worst it can do to me
Is carry some garden soil
A little nearer the sea.

'Tis the world-old way of the rain
When it comes to a mountain farm
To exact for a present gain
A little of future harm.

And the harm is none too sure,
For when all that was rotted rich
Shall be in the end scoured poor,
When my garden has gone down ditch,

Some force has but to apply,
And summits shall be immersed,
The bottom of seas raised dry–
The slope of the earth reversed.

Then all I need do is run
To the other end of the slope,
And on tracts laid new to the sun,
Begin all over to hope.

Some worn old tool of my own
Will be turned up by the plow,

The wood of it changed to stone,
But as ready to wield as now.

May my application so close
To so endless a repetition
Not make me tired and morose
And resentful of man's condition.

A ROADSIDE STAND

The little old house was out with a little new shed
In front at the edge of the road where the traffic sped,
A roadside stand that too pathetically plead,
It would not be fair to say for a dole of bread,
But for some of the money, the cash, whose flow sup-
    ports
The flower of cities from sinking and withering faint.
The polished traffic passed with a mind ahead,
Or if ever aside a moment, then out of sorts
At having the landscape marred with the artless paint
Of signs that with N turned wrong and S turned wrong
Offered for sale wild berries in wooden quarts,
Or crook-necked golden squash with silver warts,
Or beauty rest in a beautiful mountain scene.
You have the money, but if you want to be mean,
Why keep your money (this crossly), and go along.
The hurt to the scenery wouldn't be my complaint
So much as the trusting sorrow of what is unsaid:
Here far from the city we make our roadside stand
And ask for some city money to feel in hand
To try if it will not make our being expand,
And give us the life of the moving pictures' promise
That the party in power is said to be keeping from us.

It is in the news that all these pitiful kin
Are to be bought out and mercifully gathered in
To live in villages next to the theatre and store

Where they won't have to think for themselves any
    more;
While greedy good-doers, beneficent beasts of prey,
Swarm over their lives enforcing benefits
That are calculated to soothe them out of their wits,
And by teaching them how to sleep the sleep all day,
Destroy their sleeping at night the ancient way.

Sometimes I feel myself I can hardly bear
The thought of so much childish longing in vain,
The sadness that lurks near the open window there,
That waits all day in almost open prayer
For the squeal of brakes, the sound of a stopping car,
Of all the thousand selfish cars that pass,
Just one to inquire what a farmer's prices are.
And one did stop, but only to plow up grass
In using the yard to back and turn around;
And another to ask the way to where it was bound;
And another to ask could they sell it a gallon of gas
They couldn't (this crossly): they had none, didn't it
    see?

No, in country money, the country scale of gain,
The requisite lift of spirit has never been found,
Or so the voice of the country seems to complain.
I can't help owning the great relief it would be
To put these people at one stroke out of their pain.
And then next day as I come back into the sane,
I wonder how I should like you to come to me
And offer to put me gently out of my pain.

DEPARTMENTAL

An ant on the table cloth
Ran into a dormant moth
Of many times his size.
He showed not the least surprise.
His business wasn't with such.
He gave it scarcely a touch,
And was off on his duty run.
Yet if he encountered one
Of the hive's enquiry squad
Whose work is to find out God
And the nature of time and space,
He would put him onto the case.
Ants are a curious race;
One crossing with hurried tread
The body of one of their dead
Isn't given a moment's arrest –
Seems not even impressed.
But he no doubt reports to any
With whom he crosses antennae,
And they no doubt report
To the higher up at court.
Then word goes forth in Formic:
"Death's come to Jerry McCormic,
Our selfless forager Jerry.
Will the special Janizary
Whose office it is to bury
The dead of the commissary

Go bring him home to his people.
Lay him in state on a sepal.
Wrap him for shroud in a petal.
Embalm him with ichor of nettle.
This is the word of your Queen."
And presently on the scene
Appears a solemn mortician;
And taking formal position
With feelers calmly atwiddle,
Seizes the dead by the middle,
And heaving him high in air,
Carries him out of there.
No one stands round to stare.
It is nobody else's affair.

It couldn't be called ungentle.
But how thoroughly departmental.

THE OLD BARN AT THE BOTTOM
OF THE FOGS

Where's this barn's house? It never had a house,
Or joined with sheds in ring-around a dooryard.
The hunter scuffling leaves goes by at dusk,
The gun reversed that he went out with shouldered.
The harvest moon and then the hunter's moon.
Well, the moon after that came one at last
To close this outpost barn and close the season.
The fur-thing, muff-thing, rocking in and out
Across the threshold in the twilight fled him.
He took the props down used for propping open,
And set them up again for propping shut,
The wide-spread double doors two stories high.
The advantage-disadvantage of these doors
Was that tramp taking sanctuary there
Must leave them unlocked to betray his presence.
They could be locked but from the outside only.
There is a fellow on the ocean now
Or down a mine or at the mill (I met him)
Who slept there in a mow of meadow hay
One night (he told me). And the barn he meant
Was the one I meant. Our details agreed.
We said Well twice to what we had in common,
The old barn at the bottom of the fogs.
Its only windows were the crevices
All up and down it. So that waking there
Next morning to the light of day was more

Like waking in a cage of silver bars.
Its locks were props – and that reminded him.
Trust him to have his bitter politics
Against his unacquaintances the rich
Who sleep in houses of their own, though mortgaged.
Conservatives, they don't know what to save.
Consider what they treasure under glass,
Yet leave such lovely shafts outdoors to perish.
Would someone only act in time we yet
Might see them on a rack like famous oars,
Their label Prop-locks, only specimens
In chestnut now become a precious wood
As relic of a vanished race of trees –
When these go there will be none to replace them.
Yes, right I was the locks were props outside;
And it had almost given him troubled dreams
To think that though he could not lock himself in,
The cheapest tramp that came along that way
Could mischievously lock him in to stay.

ON THE HEART'S BEGINNING TO
CLOUD THE MIND

Something I saw or thought I saw
In the desert at midnight in Utah,
Looking out of my lower berth
At moonlit sky and moonlit earth.
The sky had here and there a star;
The earth had a single light afar,
A flickering, human pathetic light,
That was maintained against the night,
It seemed to me, by the people there,
With a God-forsaken brute despair.
It would flutter and fall in half an hour
Like the last petal off a flower.
But my heart was beginning to cloud my mind.
I knew a tale of a better kind.
That far light flickers because of trees.
The people can burn it as long as they please:
And when their interests in it end,
They can leave it to someone else to tend.
Come back that way a summer hence,
I should find it no more no less intense.
I pass, but scarcely pass no doubt,
When one will say "Let us put it out."
The other without demur agrees.
They can keep it burning as long as they please;
They can put it out whenever they please.
One looks out last from the darkened room

At the shiny desert with spots of gloom
That might be people and are but cedar,
Have no purpose, have no leader,
Have never made the first move to assemble,
And so are nothing to make her tremble.
She can think of places that are not thus
Without indulging a "Not for us!"
Life is not so sinister-grave.
Matter of fact has made them brave.
He is husband, she is wife.
She fears not him, they fear not life.
They know where another light has been,
And more than one to theirs akin,
But earlier out for bed tonight,
So lost on me in my surface flight.

This I saw when waking late,
Going by at a railroad rate,
Looking through wreaths of engine smoke
Far into the lives of other folk.

THE FIGURE IN THE DOORWAY

The grade surmounted, we were riding high
Through level mountains nothing to the eye
But scrub oak, scrub oak and the lack of earth
That kept the oaks from getting any girth.
But as through the monotony we ran,
We came to where there was a living man.
His great gaunt figure filled his cabin door,
And had he fallen inward on the floor,
He must have measured to the further wall.
But we who passed were not to see him fall.
The miles and miles he lived from anywhere
Were evidently something he could bear.
He stood unshaken, and if grim and gaunt,
It was not necessarily from want.
He had the oaks for heating and for light.
He had a hen, he had a pig in sight.
He had a well, he had the rain to catch.
He had a ten by twenty garden patch.
Nor did he lack for common entertainment.
That I assume was what our passing train meant.
He could look at us in our diner eating,
And if so moved uncurl a hand in greeting.

AT WOODWARD'S GARDENS

A boy, presuming on his intellect,
Once showed two little monkeys in a cage
A burning-glass they could not understand
And never could be made to understand.
Words are no good: to say it was a lens
For gathering solar rays would not have helped.
But let him show them how the weapon worked.
He made the sun a pin-point on the nose
Of first one then the other till it brought
A look of puzzled dimness to their eyes
That blinking could not seem to blink away.
They stood arms laced together at the bars,
And exchanged troubled glances over life.
One put a thoughtful hand up to his nose
As if reminded – or as if perhaps
Within a million years of an idea.
He got his purple little knuckles stung.
The already known had once more been confirmed
By psychological experiment,
And that were all the finding to announce
Had the boy not presumed too close and long.
There was a sudden flash of arm, a snatch,
And the glass was the monkeys' not the boy's.
Precipitately they retired back cage
And instituted an investigation
On their part, though without the needed insight.
They bit the glass and listened for the flavor.

They broke the handle and the binding off it.
Then none the wiser, frankly gave it up,
And having hid it in their bedding straw
Against the day of prisoners' ennui,
Came dryly forward to the bars again
To answer for themselves: Who said it mattered
What monkeys did or didn't understand?
They might not understand a burning-glass.
They might not understand the sun itself.
It's knowing what to do with things that counts.

A RECORD STRIDE

In a Vermont bedroom closet
With a door of two broad boards
And for back wall a crumbling old chimney
(And that's what their toes are towards),

I have a pair of shoes standing,
Old rivals of sagging leather,
Who once kept surpassing each other,
But now live even together.

They listen for me in the bedroom
To ask me a thing or two
About who is too old to go walking,
With too much stress on the who.

I wet one last year at Montauk
For a hat I had to save.
The other I wet at the Cliff House
In an extra-vagant wave.

Two entirely different grandchildren
Got me into my double adventure.
But when they grow up and can read this
I hope they won't take it for censure.

I touch my tongue to the shoes now
And unless my sense is at fault,

On one I can taste Atlantic,
On the other Pacific, salt.

One foot in each great ocean
Is a record stride or stretch.
The authentic shoes it was made in
I should sell for what they would fetch.

But instead I proudly devote them
To my museum and muse;
So the thick-skins needn't act thin-skinned
About being past-active shoes.

And I ask all to try to forgive me
For being as over-elated
As if I had measured the country
And got the United States stated.

TAKEN SINGLY

LOST IN HEAVEN

The clouds, the source of rain, one stormy night
Offered an opening to the source of dew;
Which I accepted with impatient sight,
Looking for my old skymarks in the blue.

But stars were scarce in that part of the sky,
And no two were of the same constellation –
No one was bright enough to identify;
So 'twas with not ungrateful consternation,

Seeing myself well lost once more, I sighed,
"Where, where in Heaven am I? But don't tell me!"
I warned the clouds, "by opening on me wide.
Let's let my heavenly lostness overwhelm me."

DESERT PLACES

Snow falling and night falling fast oh fast
In a field I looked into going past,
And the ground almost covered smooth in snow,
But a few weeds and stubble showing last.

The woods around it have it – it is theirs.
All animals are smothered in their lairs.
I am too absent-spirited to count;
The loneliness includes me unawares.

And lonely as it is that loneliness
Will be more lonely ere it will be less –
A blanker whiteness of benighted snow
With no expression, nothing to express.

They cannot scare me with their empty spaces
Between stars – on stars where no human race is.
I have it in me so much nearer home
To scare myself with my own desert places.

LEAVES COMPARED WITH FLOWERS

A tree's leaves may be ever so good,
So may its bark, so may its wood;
But unless you put the right thing to its root
It never will show much flower or fruit.

But I may be one who does not care
Ever to have tree bloom or bear.
Leaves for smooth and bark for rough,
Leaves and bark may be tree enough.

Some giant trees have bloom so small
They might as well have none at all.
Late in life I have come on fern.
Now lichens are due to have their turn.

I bade men tell me which in brief,
Which is fairer, flower or leaf.
They did not have the wit to say,
Leaves by night and flowers by day.

Leaves and bark, leaves and bark,
To lean against and hear in the dark.
Petals I may have once pursued.
Leaves are all my darker mood.

A LEAF TREADER

I have been treading on leaves all day until I am
   autumn-tired.
God knows all the color and form of leaves I have
   trodden on and mired.
Perhaps I have put forth too much strength and
   been too fierce from fear.
I have safely trodden underfoot the leaves of another year.

All summer long they were over head, more
   lifted up than I.
To come to their final place in earth they had to
   pass me by.
All summer long I thought I heard them threaten-
   ing under their breath.
And when they came it seemed with a will to
   carry me with them to death.

They spoke to the fugitive in my heart as if it
   were leaf to leaf.
They tapped at my eyelids and touched my lips
   with an invitation to grief.
But it was no reason I had to go because they
   had to go.
Now up my knee to keep on top of another year
   of snow.

ON TAKING FROM THE TOP TO
BROADEN THE BASE

Roll stones down on our head!
You squat old pyramid,
Your last good avalanche
Was long since slid.

Your top has sunk too low,
Your base has spread too wide,
For you to roll one stone
Down if you tried.

But even at the word
A pebble hit the roof,
Another shot through glass
Demanding proof.

Before their panic hands
Were fighting for the latch,
The mud came in one cold
Unleavened batch.

And none was left to prate
Of an old mountain's case
That still took from its top
To broaden its base.

THEY WERE WELCOME TO
THEIR BELIEF

Grief may have thought it was grief.
Care may have thought it was care.
They were welcome to their belief,
The over important pair.

No, it took all the snows that clung
To the low roof over his bed,
Beginning when he was young,
To induce the one snow on his head.

But whenever the roof came white
The head in the dark below
Was a shade less the color of night
A shade more the color of snow.

Grief may have thought it was grief.
Care may have thought it was care.
But neither one was the thief
Of his raven color of hair.

THE STRONG ARE SAYING NOTHING

The soil now gets a rumpling soft and damp,
And small regard to the future of any weed.
The final flat of the hoe's approval stamp
Is reserved for the bed of a few selected seed.

There is seldom more than a man to a harrowed piece.
Men work alone, their lots plowed far apart,
One stringing a chain of seed in an open crease,
And another stumbling after a halting cart.

To the fresh and black of the squares of early mould
The leafless bloom of a plum is fresh and white;
Though there's more than a doubt if the weather is not
    too cold
For the bees to come and serve its beauty aright.

Wind goes from farm to farm in wave on wave,
But carries no cry of what is hoped to be.
There may be little or much beyond the grave,
But the strong are saying nothing until they see.

THE MASTER SPEED

No speed of wind or water rushing by
But you have speed far greater. You can climb
Back up a stream of radiance to the sky,
And back through history up the stream of time.
And you were given this swiftness, not for haste,
Nor chiefly that you may go where you will,
But in the rush of everything to waste,
That you may have the power of standing still —
Off any still or moving thing you say.
Two such as you with such a master speed
Cannot be parted nor be swept away
From one another once you are agreed
That life is only life forevermore
Together wing to wing and oar to oar.

MOON COMPASSES

I stole forth dimly in the dripping pause
Between two downpours to see what there was.
And a masked moon had spread down compass rays
To a cone mountain in the midnight haze,
As if the final estimate were hers,
And as it measured in her calipers,
The mountain stood exalted in its place.
So love will take between the hands a face . . .

NEITHER OUT FAR NOR IN DEEP

The people along the sand
All turn and look one way.
They turn their back on the land.
They look at the sea all day.

As long as it takes to pass
A ship keeps raising its hull;
The wetter ground like glass
Reflects a standing gull.

The land may vary more;
But wherever the truth may be –
The water comes ashore,
And the people look at the sea.

They cannot look out far.
They cannot look in deep.
But when was that ever a bar
To any watch they keep?

VOICE WAYS

Some things are never clear.
But the weather is clear tonight,
Thanks to a clearing rain.
The mountains are brought up near,
The stars are brought out bright.
Your old sweet-cynical strain
Would come in like you here:
"So we won't say nothing is clear."

DESIGN

I found a dimpled spider, fat and white,
On a white heal-all, holding up a moth
Like a white piece of rigid satin cloth—
Assorted characters of death and blight
Mixed ready to begin the morning right,
Like the ingredients of a witches' broth—
A snow-drop spider, a flower like froth,
And dead wings carried like a paper kite.

What had that flower to do with being white,
The wayside blue and innocent heal-all?
What brought the kindred spider to that height,
Then steered the white moth thither in the night?
What but design of darkness to appall?—
If design govern in a thing so small.

ON A BIRD SINGING IN ITS SLEEP

A bird half wakened in the lunar noon
Sang half way through its little inborn tune.
Partly because it sang but once all night
And that from no especial bush's height;
Partly because it sang ventriloquist
And had the inspiration to desist
Almost before the prick of hostile ears,
It ventured less in peril than appears.
It could not have come down to us so far
Through the interstices of things ajar
On the long bead chain of repeated birth
To be a bird while we are men on earth
If singing out of sleep and dream that way
Had made it much more easily a prey.

AFTER-FLAKES

In the thick of a teeming snowfall
I saw my shadow on snow.
I turned and looked back up at the sky,
Where we still look to ask the why
Of everything below.

If I shed such a darkness,
If the reason was in me,
That shadow of mine should show in form
Against the shapeless shadow of storm,
How swarthy I must be.

I turned and looked back upward.
The whole sky was blue;
And the thick flakes floating at a pause
Were but frost knots on an airy gauze,
With the sun shining through.

CLEAR AND COLDER

Wind the season-climate mixer
In my Witches' Weather Primer
Says to make this Fall Elixir
First you let the summer simmer,
Using neither spoon nor skimmer,

Till about the right consistence.
(This like fate by stars is reckoned,
None remaining in existence
Under magnitude the second);

Then take some left-over winter
Far to north of the St. Lawrence.
Leaves to strip and branches splinter,
Bring on wind. Bring rain in torrents—
Colder than the season warrants.

Dash it with some snow for powder.
If this seems like witchcraft rather,
If this seems a witches' chowder
(All my eye and Cotton Mather!),

Wait and watch the liquor settle.
I could stand whole dayfuls of it.
Wind she brews a heady kettle.
Human beings love it—love it.
Gods above are not above it.

UNHARVESTED

A scent of ripeness from over a wall.
And come to leave the routine road
And look for what had made me stall,
There sure enough was an appletree
That had eased itself of its summer load,
And of all but its trivial foliage free,
Now breathed as light as a lady's fan.
For there there had been an apple fall
As complete as the apple had given man.
The ground was one circle of solid red.

May something go always unharvested!
May much stay out of our stated plan,
Apples or something forgotten and left,
So smelling their sweetness would be no theft.

THERE ARE ROUGHLY ZONES

We sit indoors and talk of the cold outside.
And every gust that gathers strength and heaves
Is a threat to the house. But the house has long been
    tried.
We think of the tree. If it never again has leaves,
We'll know, we say, that this was the night it died.
It is very far north, we admit, to have brought the
    peach.
What comes over a man, is it soul or mind –
That to no limits and bounds he can stay confined?
You would say his ambition was to extend the reach
Clear to the Arctic of every living kind.
Why is his nature forever so hard to teach
That though there is no fixed line between wrong and
    right,
There are roughly zones whose laws must be obeyed.
There is nothing much we can do for the tree tonight,
But we can't help feeling more than a little betrayed
That the northwest wind should rise to such a height
Just when the cold went down so many below.
The tree has no leaves and may never have them
    again.
We must wait till some months hence in the spring to
    know.
But if it is destined never again to grow,
It can blame this limitless trait in the hearts of men.

A TRIAL RUN

I said to myself almost in prayer,
It will start hair raising currents of air
When you give it the livid metal-sap.
It will make a homicidal roar.
It will shake its cast stone reef of floor.
It will gather speed till your nerves prepare
To hear it wreck in a thunder-clap.
But stand your ground
As they say in war.
It is cotter-pinned, it is bedded true.
Everything its parts can do
Has been thought out and accounted for.
Your least touch sets it going round,
And when to stop it rests with you.

NOT QUITE SOCIAL

Some of you will be glad I did what I did,
And the rest won't want to punish me too severely
For finding a thing to do that though not forbid
Yet wasn't enjoined and wasn't expected clearly.

To punish me over cruelly wouldn't be right
For merely giving you once more gentle proof
That the city's hold on a man is no more tight
Than when its walls rose higher than any roof.

You may taunt me with not being able to flee the earth.
You have me there, but loosely as I would be held.
The way of understanding is partly mirth.
I would not be taken as ever having rebelled.

And anyone is free to condemn me to death—
If he leaves it to nature to carry out the sentence.
I shall will to the common stock of air my breath
And pay a death-tax of fairly polite repentance.

PROVIDE PROVIDE

The witch that came (the withered hag)
To wash the steps with pail and rag,
Was once the beauty Abishag,

The picture pride of Hollywood.
Too many fall from great and good
For you to doubt the likelihood.

Die early and avoid the fate.
Or if predestined to die late,
Make up your mind to die in state.

Make the whole stock exchange your own!
If need be occupy a throne,
Where nobody can call *you* crone.

Some have relied on what they knew;
Others on being simply true.
What worked for them might work for you.

No memory of having starred
Atones for later disregard,
Or keeps the end from being hard.

Better to go down dignified
With boughten friendship at your side
Than none at all. Provide, provide!

TEN MILLS

TEN MILLS

Precaution

I never dared be radical when young
For fear it would make me conservative when old.

The Span of Life

The old dog barks backward without getting up.
I can remember when he was a pup.

The Wrights' Biplane

This biplane is the shape of human flight.
Its name might better be First Motor Kite.
Its makers' name –Time cannot get that wrong,
For it was writ in heaven doubly Wright.

Assertive

Let me be the one
To do what is done.

Evil Tendencies Cancel

Will the blight end the chestnut?
The farmers rather guess not.
It keeps smouldering at the roots
And sending up new shoots
Till another parasite
Shall come to end the blight.

Pertinax

Let chaos storm!
Let cloud shapes swarm!
I wait for form.

Waspish

On glossy wires artistically bent,
He draws himself up to his full extent.
His natty wings with self-assurance perk.
His stinging quarters menacingly work.
Poor egotist, he has no way of knowing
But he's as good as anybody going.

One Guess

He has dust in his eyes and a fan for a wing,
A leg akimbo with which he can sing,
And a mouthful of dye stuff instead of a sting.

The Hardship of Accounting

Never ask of money spent
Where the spender thinks it went.
Nobody was ever meant
To remember or invent
What he did with every cent.

Not All There

I turned to speak to God
About the world's despair;
But to make bad matters worse
I found God wasn't there.

God turned to speak to me
(Don't anybody laugh)
God found I wasn't there—
At least not over half.

In Dives' Dive

It is late at night and still I am losing,
But still I am steady and unaccusing.

As long as the Declaration guards
My right to be equal in number of cards,

It is nothing to me who runs the Dive.
Let's have a look at another five.

THE OUTLANDS

THE VINDICTIVES

You like to hear about gold.
A king filled his prison room
As full as the room could hold
To the top of his reach on the wall
With every known shape of the stuff.
'Twas to buy himself off his doom.
But it wasn't ransom enough.
His captors accepted it all,
But didn't let go of the king.
They made him send out a call
To his subjects to gather them more.
And his subjects wrung all they could wring
Out of temple and palace and store.
But when there seemed no more to bring,
His captors convicted the king
Of once having started a war,
And strangled the wretch with a string.

But really that gold was not half
That a king might have hoped to compel—
Not a half, not a third, not a tithe.
The king had scarce ceased to writhe,
When hate gave a terrible laugh,
Like a manhole opened to Hell.
If gold pleased the conqueror, well,
That gold should be the one thing
The conqueror henceforth should lack.

They gave no more thought to the king.
All joined in the game of hide-gold.
They swore all the gold should go back
Deep into the earth whence it came.
Their minds ran on cranny and crack.
All joined in the maddening game.
The tale is still boastingly told
Of many a treasure by name
That vanished into the black
And put out its light for the foe.

That self-sack and self-overthrow,
That was the splendidest sack
Since the forest Germans sacked Rome
And took the gold candlesticks home.

One Inca prince on the rack,
And late in his last hour alive,
Told them in what lake to dive
To seek what they seemed so to want.
They dived and nothing was found.
He told them to dive till they drowned.
The whole fierce conquering pack
Hunted and tortured and raged.
There were suns of story and vaunt
They searched for into Brazil
Their tongues hanging out unassuaged.

But the conquered grew meek and still.
They slowly and silently aged.

They kept their secrets and died,
Maliciously satisfied.
One knew of a burial hole
In the floor of a tribal cave,
Where under deep ash and charcoal
And cracked bones, human and beast,
The midden of feast upon feast,
Was coiled in its last resting grave
The great treasure wanted the most,
The great thousand-linked gold chain,
Each link of a hundred weight,
That once between post and post
(In-leaning under the strain),
And looped ten times back and forth,
Had served as a palace gate.
Some said it had gone to the coast,
Some over the mountains east,
Some into the country north,
On the backs of a single-file host,
Commanded by one sun-priest,
And raising a dust with a train
Of flashing links in the sun.
No matter what some may say.
(The saying is never done.)
There bright in the filth it lay
Untarnished by rust and decay.
And be all plunderers curst.

"The best way to hate is the worst.
'Tis to find what the hated need,

Never mind of what actual worth,
And wipe that out of the earth.
Let them die of unsatisfied greed,
Of unsatisfied love of display,
Of unsatisfied love of the high,
Unvulgar, unsoiled, and ideal.
Let their trappings be taken away.
Let them suffer starvation and die
Of being brought down to the real."

THE BEARER OF EVIL TIDINGS

The bearer of evil tidings,
When he was halfway there,
Remembered that evil tidings
Were a dangerous thing to bear.

So when he came to the parting
Where one road led to the throne
And one went off to the mountains
And into the wild unknown,

He took the one to the mountains.
He ran through the Vale of Cashmere,
He ran through rhododendrons
Till he came to the land of Pamir.

And there in a precipice valley
A girl of his age he met
Took him home to her bower,
Or he might be running yet.

She taught him her tribe's religion:
How ages and ages since
A princess en route from China
To marry a Persian prince

Had been found with child; and her army
Had come to a troubled halt.

And though a god was the father
And nobody else at fault,

It had seemed discreet to remain there
And neither go on nor back.
So they stayed and declared a village
There in the land of the Yak.

And the child that came of the princess
Established a royal line,
And his mandates were given heed to
Because he was born divine.

And that was why there were people
On one Himalayan shelf;
And the bearer of evil tidings
Decided to stay there himself.

At least he had this in common
With the race he chose to adopt:
They had both of them had their reasons
For stopping where they had stopped.

As for his evil tidings,
Belshazzar's overthrow,
Why hurry to tell Belshazzar
What soon enough he would know?

IRIS BY NIGHT

One misty evening, one another's guide,
We two were groping down a Malvern side
The last wet fields and dripping hedges home.
There came a moment of confusing lights,
Such as according to belief in Rome
Were seen of old at Memphis on the heights
Before the fragments of a former sun
Could concentrate anew and rise as one.
Light was a paste of pigment in our eyes.
And then there was a moon and then a scene
So watery as to seem submarine;
In which we two stood saturated, drowned.
The clover-mingled rowan on the ground
Had taken all the water it could as dew,
And still the air was saturated too,
Its airy pressure turned to water weight.
Then a small rainbow like a trellis gate,
A very small moon-made prismatic bow,
Stood closely over us through which to go.
And then we were vouchsafed the miracle
That never yet to other two befell
And I alone of us have lived to tell.
A wonder! Bow and rainbow as it bent,
Instead of moving with us as we went,
(To keep the pots of gold from being found)
It lifted from its dewy pediment
Its two mote-swimming many-colored ends,

And gathered them together in a ring.
And we stood in it softly circled round
From all division time or foe can bring
In a relation of elected friends.

BUILD SOIL

BUILD SOIL–A POLITICAL PASTORAL

Why Tityrus! But you've forgotten me.
I'm Meliboeus the potato man,
The one you had the talk with, you remember,
Here on this very campus years ago.
Hard times have struck me and I'm on the move.
I've had to give my interval farm up
For interest, and I've bought a mountain farm
For nothing down, all-out-doors of a place,
All woods and pasture only fit for sheep.
But sheep is what I'm going into next.
I'm done forever with potato crops
At thirty cents a bushel. Give me sheep.
I know wool's down to seven cents a pound.
But I don't calculate to sell my wool.
I didn't my potatoes. I consumed them.
I'll dress up in sheep's clothing and eat sheep.
The Muse takes care of you. You live by writing
Your poems on a farm and call that farming.
Oh I don't blame you. I say take life easy.
I should myself, only I don't know how.
But have some pity on us who have to work.
Why don't you use your talents as a writer
To advertise our farms to city buyers,
Or else write something to improve food prices.
Get in a poem toward the next election.

Oh Meliboeus, I have half a mind

To take a writing hand in politics.
Before now poetry has taken notice
Of wars, and what are wars but politics
Transformed from chronic to acute and bloody?

I may be wrong, but Tityrus to me
The times seem revolutionary bad.

The question is whether they've reached a depth
Of desperation that would warrant poetry's
Leaving love's alternations, joy and grief,
The weather's alternations, summer and winter,
Our age-long theme, for the uncertainty
Of judging who is a contemporary liar—
Who in particular, when all alike
Get called as much in clashes of ambition.
Life may be tragically bad, and I
Make bold to sing it so, but do I dare
Name names and tell you who by name is wicked?
Whittier's luck with Skipper Ireson awes me.
Many men's luck with Greatest Washington
(Who sat for Stuart's portrait, but who sat
Equally for the nation's Constitution).
I prefer to sing safely in the realm
Of types, composite and imagined people:
To affirm there is such a thing as evil
Personified, but ask to be excused
From saying on a jury "Here's the guilty."

I doubt if you're convinced the times are bad.

I keep my eye on Congress, Meliboeus.
They're in the best position of us all
To know if anything is very wrong.
I mean they could be trusted to give the alarm
If earth were thought about to change its axis,
Or a star coming to dilate the sun.
As long as lightly all their live-long sessions,
Like a yard full of school boys out at recess
Before their plays and games were organized,
They yelling mix tag, hide-and-seek, hop-scotch,
And leap frog in each other's way,—all's well.
Let newspapers profess to fear the worst!
Nothing's portentous, I am reassured.

Is socialism needed, do you think?

We have it now. For socialism is
An element in any government.
There's no such thing as socialism pure—
Except as an abstraction of the mind.
There's only democratic socialism
Monarchic socialism—oligarchic,
The last being what they seem to have in Russia.
You often get it most in monarchy,
Least in democracy. In practice, pure,
I don't know what it would be. No one knows.
I have no doubt like all the loves when
Philosophized together into one—
One sickness of the body and the soul.

Thank God our practice holds the loves apart
Beyond embarrassing self-consciousness
Where natural friends are met, where dogs are kept,
Where women pray with priests. There is no love.
There's only love of men and women, love
Of children, love of friends, of men, of God,
Divine love, human love, parental love,
Roughly discriminated for the rough.

Poetry, itself once more, is back in love.

Pardon the analogy, my Meliboeus,
For sweeping me away. Let's see, where was I?

But don't you think more should be socialized
Than is?

       What should you mean by socialized?

Made good for everyone – things like inventions –
Made so we all should get the good of them –
All, not just great exploiting businesses.

We sometimes only get the bad of them.
In your sense of the word ambition has
Been socialized – the first propensity
To be attempted. Greed may well come next.
But the worst one of all to leave uncurbed,
Unsocialized, is ingenuity:

Which for no sordid self-aggrandizement,
For nothing but its own blind satisfaction
(In this it is as much like hate as love)
Works in the dark as much against as for us.
Even while we talk some chemist at Columbia
Is stealthily contriving wool from jute
That when let loose upon the grazing world
Will put ten thousand farmers out of sheep.
Everyone asks for freedom for himself,
The man free love, the business man free trade,
The writer and talker free speech and free press.
Political ambition has been taught,
By being punished back, it is not free:
It must at some point gracefully refrain.
Greed has been taught a little abnegation
And shall be more before we're done with it.
It is just fool enough to think itself
Self-taught. But our brute snarling and lashing
    taught it.
None shall be as ambitious as he can.
None should be as ingenious as he could,
Not if I had my say. Bounds should be set
To ingenuity for being so cruel
In bringing change unheralded on the unready.

I elect you to put the curb on it.

Were I dictator, I'll tell you what I'd do.

What should you do?

>   I'd let things take their course
> And then I'd claim the credit for the outcome.

You'd make a sort of safety-first dictator.

Don't let the things I say against myself
Betray you into taking sides against me,
Or it might get you into trouble with me.
I'm not afraid to prophesy the future,
And be judged by the outcome, Meliboeus.
Listen and I will take my dearest risk.
We're always too much out or too much in.
At present from a cosmical dilation
We're so much out that the odds are against
Our ever getting inside in again.
But inside in is where we've got to get.
My friends all know I'm interpersonal.
But long before I'm interpersonal
Away 'way down inside I'm personal.
Just so before we're international
We're national and act as nationals.
The colors are kept unmixed on the palette,
Or better on dish plates all around the room,
So the effect when they are mixed on canvas
May seem almost exclusively designed.
Some minds are so confounded intermental
They remind me of pictures on a palette
"Look at what happened. Surely some God pinxit.
Come look at my significant mud pie."

It's hard to tell which is the worse abhorrence
Whether it's persons pied or nations pied.
Don't let me seem to say the exchange, the encounter,
May not be the important thing at last.
It well may be. We meet – I don't say when –
But must bring to the meeting the maturest,
The longest-saved-up, raciest, localest
We have strength of reserve in us to bring.

Tityrus, sometimes I'm perplexed myself
To find the good of commerce. Why should I
Have to sell you my apples and buy yours?
It can't be just to give the robber a chance
To catch them and take toll of them in transit.
Too mean a thought to get much comfort out of.
I figure that like any bandying
Of words or toys, it ministers to health.
It very likely quickens and refines us.

To market 'tis our destiny to go.
But much as in the end we bring for sale there
There is still more we never bring or should bring;
More that should be kept back – the soil for instance
In my opinion, – though we both know poets
Who fall all over each other to bring soil
And even subsoil and hardpan to market.
To sell the hay off, let alone the soil,
Is an unpardonable sin in farming.
The moral is, make a late start to market.
Let me preach to you, will you Meliboeus?

Preach on. I thought you were already preaching.
But preach and see if I can tell the difference.

Needless to say to you, my argument
Is not to lure the city to the country.
Let those possess the land and only those,
Who love it with a love so strong and stupid
That they may be abused and taken advantage of
And made fun of by business, law and art;
They still hang on. That so much of the earth's
Unoccupied need not make us uneasy.
We don't pretend to complete occupancy.
The world's one globe, human society
Another softer globe that slightly flattened
Rests on the world, and clinging slowly rolls.
We have our own round shape to keep unbroken.
The world's size has no more to do with us
Than has the universe's. We are balls,
We are round from the same source of roundness.
We are both round because the mind is round,
Because all reasoning is in a circle.
At least that's why the universe is round.

If what you're preaching is a line of conduct,
Just what am I supposed to do about it?
Reason in circles?

                    No, refuse to be
Seduced back to the land by any claim

The land may seem to have on man to use it.
Let none assume to till the land but farmers.
I only speak to you as one of them.
You shall go to your run-out mountain farm,
Poor cast-away of commerce, and so live
That none shall ever see you come to market—
Not for a long long time. Plant, breed, produce,
But what you raise or grow, why feed it out,
Eat it or plow it under where it stands
To build the soil. For what is more accursed
Than an impoverished soil pale and metallic?
What cries more to our kind for sympathy?
I'll make a compact with you, Meliboeus,
To match you deed for deed and plan for plan.
Friends crowd around me with their five year plans
That Soviet Russia has made fashionable.
You come to me and I'll unfold to you
A five year plan I call so, not because
It takes ten years or so to carry out,
Rather because it took five years at least
To think it out. Come close, let us conspire—
In self-restraint, if in restraint of trade.
You will go to your run-out mountain farm
And do what I command you. I take care
To command only what you meant to do
Anyway. That is my style of dictator.
Build soil. Turn the farm in upon itself
Until it can contain itself no more,
But sweating-full, drips wine and oil a little.

I will go to my run-out social mind
And be as unsocial with it as I can.
The thought I have, and my first impulse is
To take to market–I will turn it under.
The thought from that thought–I will turn it under.
And so on to the limit of my nature.
We are too much out, and if we won't draw in
We shall be driven in. I was brought up
A state-rights free-trade Democrat. What's that?
An inconsistency. The state shall be
Laws to itself, it seems, and yet have no
Control of what it sells or what it buys.
Suppose someone comes near me who in rate
Of speech and thinking is so much my better
I am imposed on, silenced and discouraged.
Do I submit to being supplied by him
As the more economical producer,
More wonderful, more beautiful producer?
No I unostentatiously move off
Far enough for my thought-flow to resume.
Thought product and food product are to me
Nothing compared to the producing of them.
I sent you once a song with the refrain:

> Let me be the one
> To do what is done–

My share at least lest I be empty-idle.
Keep off each other and keep each other off.
You see the beauty of my proposal is
It needn't wait on general revolution.

I bid you to a one-man revolution–
The only revolution that is coming.
We're too unseparate out among each other–
With goods to sell and notions to impart.
A youngster comes to me with half a quatrain
To ask me if I think it worth the pains
Of working out the rest, the other half.
I am brought guaranteed young prattle poems
Made publicly in school, above suspicion
Of plagiarism and help of cheating parents.
We congregate embracing from distrust
As much as love, and too close in to strike
And be so very striking. Steal away
The song says. Steal away and stay away.
Don't join too many gangs. Join few if any.
Join the United States and join the family–
But not much in between unless a college.
Is it a bargain, Shepherd Meliboeus?

Probably but you're far too fast and strong
For my mind to keep working in your presence.
I can tell better after I get home,
Better a month from now when cutting posts
Or mending fence it all comes back to me
What I was thinking when you interrupted
My life-train logic. I agree with you
We're too unseparate. And going home
From company means coming to our senses.

TO A THINKER

The last step taken found your heft
Decidedly upon the left.
One more would throw you on the right.
Another still – you see your plight.
You call this thinking, but it's walking.
Not even that, it's only rocking,
Or weaving like a stabled horse:
From force to matter and back to force,
From form to content and back to form,
From norm to crazy and back to norm,
From bound to free and back to bound,
From sound to sense and back to sound.
So back and forth. It almost scares
A man the way things come in pairs.
Just now you're off democracy
(With a polite regret to be),
And leaning on dictatorship;
But if you will accept the tip,
In less than no time, tongue and pen,
You'll be a democrat again.
A reasoner and good as such,
Don't let it bother you too much
If it makes you look helpless please
And a temptation to the tease.
Suppose you've no direction in you,
I don't see but you must continue
To use the gift you do possess,

And sway with reason more or less.
I own I never really warmed
To the reformer or reformed,
And yet conversion has its place
Not half way down the scale of grace.
So if you find you must repent
From side to side in argument,
At least don't use your mind too hard,
But trust my instinct – I'm a bard.

AFTERTHOUGHT

A MISSIVE MISSILE

Some one in ancient Mas d'Azil
Once took a little pebble wheel
And dotted it with red for me,
And sent it to me years and years—
A million years to be precise—
Across the barrier of ice:
Two round dots and a ripple streak,
So vivid as to seem to speak.
But what imperfectly appears
Is whether the two dots were tears,
Two tear drops, one for either eye,
And the wave line a shaken sigh.
But no, the color used is red.
Not tears but drops of blood instead.
The line must be a jagged blade.
The sender must have had to die,
And wanted someone now to know
His death was sacrificial-votive.
So almost clear and yet obscure.
If only anyone were sure
A motive then was still a motive.
O you who bring this to my hand,
You are no common messenger
(Your badge of office is a spade).
It grieves me to have had you stand
So long for nothing. No reply—
There is no answer, I'm afraid,

Across the icy barrier
For my obscure petitioner.
Suppose his ghost is standing by
Importunate to give the hint
And be successfully conveyed.
How anyone can fail to see
Where perfectly in form and tint
The metaphor, the symbol lies!
Why will I not analogize?
(I do too much in some men's eyes.)
Oh slow uncomprehending me,
Enough to make a spirit moan
Or rustle in a bush or tree.
I have the ochre-written flint,
The two dots and the ripple line.
The meaning of it is unknown,
Or else I fear entirely mine,
All modern, nothing ancient in't,
Unsatisfying to us each.
Far as we aim our signs to reach,
Far as we often make them reach,
Across the soul-from-soul abyss,
There is an aeon-limit set
Beyond which they are doomed to miss.
Two souls may be too widely met.
That sad-with-distance river beach
With mortal longing may beseech;
It cannot speak as far as this.

A Further Range

Frost, Robert

DATE DUE

PRINTED IN U.S.A.